Contemporary Hispanic Americans

LUIS RODRIGUEZ

BY
MICHAEL SCHWARTZ

RSVP

RAINTREE
STECK-VAUGHN
P U B L I S H E R S
The Steck-Vaughn Company

Austin, Texas

Published by Raintree Steck-Vaughn, an imprint of Steck-Vaughn Company
Produced by Mega-Books, Inc.
Design and Art Direction by Michaelis/Carpelis Design Associates
Cover photo: Courtesy of ©Donna DeCesare 1996

Library of Congress Cataloging-in-Publication Data
Schwartz, Michael.
  Luis Rodriguez/Michael Schwartz.
    p. cm. — (Contemporary Hispanic Americans)
  Includes bibliographical references (p. 47) and index.
    Summary: Narrates the life of the Hispanic-American author of *Always Running* who had been a gang member and now speaks, writes, publishes, and works with youth organizations.
  ISBN 0-8172-3990-1 (Hardcover)
  ISBN 0-8172-6879-0 (Softcover)
    1. Rodriguez, Luis J., 1954–   —Biography—Juvenile literature.
2. Authors, American—20th century—Biography—Juvenile literature.
3. Hispanic Americans—Biography—Juvenile literature.
[1. Rodriguez, Luis J., 1954—   2. Authors, American.
3. Hispanic Americans—Biography.]
I. Title. II. Series.
PS3568. 034879Z88   1997
818' .5409—dc20   96-28450
[B]   CIP
                                   AC
Printed and bound in the United States.

1 2 3 4 5 6 7 8 9 LB 00 99 98 97 96

Photo credits: Courtesy of Luis J. Rodriguez: pp. 4, 8, 10, 13, 14, 17, 23, 27, 30, 35, 39, 41, 42, 45; Courtesy of Simon & Schuster: p. 7; Courtesy of ©Donna DeCesare: pp. 18, 25, 28; UPI/Corbis-Bettmann: pp. 21, 36; The Image Works/©Joe Sohm/Chromosohm 1990: p. 32.

Contents

Chapter One

TWO WAYS TO BE A WARRIOR

A ninth grader nervously raised her hand to ask a question in the school auditorium. "What do you do when you are worried about someone close to you who . . . ?" Her voice choked with emotion as she began to cry, and all heads in the auditorium turned.

"Is someone you know getting into this life?" Luis J. Rodriguez asked the girl.

She nodded. Luis looked at her for a few moments, then nodded his head in response. He seemed to understand the girl's feelings.

Luis J. Rodriguez had come to inner-city Hartford High School on this day to talk about his life. Twenty years earlier, he had been a member of a gang in East Los Angeles. He had hurt people, been shot at, been

In 1995 Luis J. Rodriguez gave a speech to 700 Milwaukee, Wisconsin high school students about his escape from gang life.

addicted to drugs, and had served time in jail. He and his friends had a special name for their experiences. They called it *La Vida Loca*—"the crazy life." By the time Luis was 18 years old, 25 of his friends had died due to violence. Somehow Luis not only survived *La Vida Loca* but also found a way to make a difference in the lives of others as a widely praised writer, journalist, and speaker.

"What you are talking about is very difficult," he told the girl in the auditorium. "The important thing is for you to try to be there for your friend. Try to understand what they are going through. Don't abandon them. If you can, keep them surrounded with friends and family, and don't give up on them."

Luis Rodriguez knows firsthand the dangers young people face in gangs. He knows he was lucky, but also believes that what saved him was finding something worthwhile in himself—something worth living for. He discovered that words were powerful tools that he could use to help himself and others. He realized there was a powerful voice inside him. Because of the power of words, Luis grew up to have a family and become a writer. He has been a factory worker as well as a newspaper reporter, an award-winning poet, a journalist, and a publisher.

However, as Luis entered his mid-30s, he saw his teenage son, Ramiro, having trouble at school, getting into fights, and facing pressures to join a neighborhood gang. It made Luis sad to see his son going through the dangers and difficulties that he had only barely managed to escape himself. Ramiro's problems made Luis feel a deep concern, not only for his son but for all young people growing up surrounded by gangs, drug addiction, and violence.

Luis decided to write the story of his life, the bad and the good, in order to share his experience with his son. He hoped Ramiro could avoid some of the mistakes that he had made.

He also wanted readers to understand and care about what is happening to many young people in cities and small towns today. He wanted to explain

"An absolutely unique work: richly literary and poetic, yet urgent and politically explosive at the same time.... A permanent testament to human courage and transcendence."
—— Jonathan Kozol, author of Savage Inequalities

ALWAYS RUNNING
LA VIDA LOCA:
GANG DAYS
IN L.A.

LUIS J. RODRIGUEZ

Reviewers praised Luis's memoir, Always Running. After the book was published, Luis had the opportunity to speak to more than 70 million people through TV and radio appearances.

that young people involved in gangs are not monsters but rather human beings with problems.

Luis titled his book *Always Running*. The many years he had spent working on poetry and learning the craft of writing paid off. Educators and critics wrote to newspapers explaining how they felt Luis's story was truthful, influential, and written with the skill and power of an artist. Before *Always Running*, very few people had written so authentically about the lives of gang members.

With the success of *Always Running*, Luis appeared on national television and radio programs and was

A visit to an elementary school in Atlanta, Georgia.

invited to travel across the country and even to Europe. In almost every city he went to, however, he also spent time visiting and talking with kids in youth groups, community centers, and schools, such as Hartford High School. He wanted to reach kids in trouble and to be an example of an older person who had faced and survived the same problems they were facing.

"If you saw me 20 years ago," he told the students at Hartford High School, "you wouldn't like me, and you'd probably stay away. I never said nothing to no one. I was cool, I was hard, I was tough, and I was very angry. I thought of myself as a kind of warrior. I didn't care if I died or who I brought down with me.

"When I almost died, it made me see things differently. I had an older friend who told me that there are two ways to be a warrior—to be a destroyer and die like one, or to create and live like one.

"The way to live like a warrior is to find the things that are important to you—in my case it was expression and writing—and dedicate your life to it. That's what I decided to do, and that's what kept me alive."

Luis told a reporter that when he visits schools and community centers, he prefers to have a conversation with kids rather than make a speech to them. At Hartford High School, he encouraged students to ask him questions. One boy asked, "What was it like to be in jail?"

"It was terrible," Luis said. "The worst part was that it felt like I lost whatever little bit of control I

Signing a book for a fan in 1994 in Washington, D.C.

thought I had. In jail you can't choose anything—when you eat, what you eat, when you watch TV, or who you talk to. It was probably the hardest time of my life."

Another boy asked, "Why did you let your son join a gang?"

"You're asking a very hard question," Luis replied. "No father would let his son be in a gang, but it isn't a father's choice. Can a father really stop a son from doing anything? A father can listen, understand, give advice, give help, but he can't live his son's life for him. My son has to make his own way, make his own decisions, like I had to make mine. The best I can do is share what I know, respect him, and be there. He's old enough now."

Another student asked, "How did you get to be a writer? Were you always good at it?"

"No. It never came easy for me. I struggled a lot with language. We spoke Spanish at home but weren't allowed to use it in school. I started school without knowing any English, and got put in the back of the classroom and forgotten. So my Spanish and my English were both bad. I never thought in a million years that I would win literary awards or become a publisher or do any of the things I do. It's a very interesting story how I grew up and ended up here today. . . ."

Chapter *Two*

CROSSING THE BORDER

"**W**e're never going back to Mexico," Alfonso Rodriguez told his wife Maria Estela. "I'd rather starve in Los Angeles than go back there."

For years, Luis's father had been determined to bring his family to the United States. When Luis's mother was about to give birth to Luis, Alfonso quickly drove her across the Mexican border into Texas. At that time, many Mexican parents who wanted their children to be able to enter into the United States freely—as U.S. citizens—did this. Luis was born at St. Joseph's Maternity Hospital in El Paso, Texas, on July 9, 1954. Soon after mother and baby were released from the hospital, the Rodriguez family had to return to their home in Ciudad Juarez, just over the border.

Alfonso Rodriguez was an educated man who was interested in art and politics. He was principal of a high school in Ciudad Juarez. Though this was a

Luis's father, Alfonso, with his oldest son, Alberto, in Mexico in 1949.

highly respected position, he found many frustrations in trying to carry out his work. The local government held back money that the school needed. His insistence on providing funds for children's education brought him into conflict with government officials and made him some powerful enemies.

Mr. Rodriguez was determined to come up with creative ways to get money for the school to operate. For example, he had a friend who was a successful artist. She would regularly exhibit and sell her work, then donate a portion of her earnings to the school. Mr. Rodriguez would contribute some of his own money to his friend so that she could buy art supplies to complete her paintings. Another way he got money for the school was by having the iron fence around the schoolyard taken down and sold for scrap.

One day Mr. Rodriguez received an invitation to

come to the United States to take part in a special program for Mexican professional people to learn English at Indiana University, in Bloomington. He accepted the invitation, but while he was away, some unfriendly school and government officials plotted to have him removed from his position. He was accused of stealing school funds. This couldn't have been farther from the truth.

Shortly after he returned to Mexico, Mr. Rodriguez was taken to the city jail. He was imprisoned for several months without being allowed to see a judge

Here, Luis poses with siblings in Los Angeles in 1957. Left to right, brother José Rene, sister Ana Virginia, and Luis (age 3).

or have visitors. Luis remembers his father telling him stories about having to eat scraps of food from a rusted can. After a long trial, he was found innocent, but he no longer had his job.

This was the last straw. Mr. Rodriguez was more determined than ever to take his family to California. He loved the United States and its promise of a better life, and he was angry and upset with what had happened to him in Mexico.

In 1956 Mr. and Mrs. Rodriguez and their three children, four-year-old José Rene, two-year-old Luis, and one-year-old Ana moved from Ciudad Juarez to Los Angeles, California. The Rodriguez family settled in and around South Central Los Angeles. Another sister, Gloria, was born two years later. Luis recalls growing up in a neighborhood filled with banana and avocado trees, engine parts, and splintered wood and wire fences. He remembers hearing the sounds of factory whistles mixed with the calls of roosters, goats, and dogs.

According to Luis, his mother had never wanted to leave Mexico. She only agreed to go because she wanted to be with her family. From the beginning, the Rodriguez family found their new life in the United States to be a struggle. To make money, Mrs. Rodriguez worked long hours as a housecleaner and later as a seamstress in garment factories.

Mr. Rodriguez's education and experience were of little use in helping him get a job in the United

States. Luis remembers his father taking whatever work he could get. At different times Mr. Rodriguez worked in a paint factory, in a dog-food factory, as a construction worker, and as a door-to-door salesman selling insurance, Bibles, and kitchenware. None of these jobs lasted for very long, and Mr. Rodriguez was often out of work.

In 1961, when Luis was six, he entered the first grade at the 109th Street Elementary School. Luis and his older brother José had a difficult time because they could not speak English. During the early 1960s, children who did not speak English were often overlooked or grouped with learning-disabled children. For example, José had to repeat first grade, then he was assigned to a class with English-speaking children who were mentally retarded.

"I remember my first-grade teacher being nice," said Luis, "but she didn't know what to do with me. She put me in the back of the room in a corner. For almost that whole year all I did was sit in that corner and build with blocks. I ended up being very shy and afraid of everyone and everything. I was also lonely, so I would keep myself company, playing things out and telling myself stories in my head."

The next year, a big change occurred for the Rodriguez family. Luis's father was hired as a substitute Spanish teacher at a high school in Woodland Hills. The family moved to a house in the

Luis's first-grade class at the 109th Street Elementary School in South Central Los Angeles. Luis is six and can be seen in the top left corner.

suburb of Reseda, in the San Fernando Valley.

The move did not last long, though. When the school year ended, Mr. Rodriguez was not asked back. The students had complained that they could not understand what he was saying because of his heavy Spanish accent. By the end of the summer, the Rodriguez family was uprooted again. This time they moved in with relatives temporarily, then found themselves in the Las Lomas **barrio** (a mostly Mexican neighborhood) in South San Gabriel, one of the many towns that surround Los Angeles.

At about this time, when Luis was 11 years old, he saw something frightening that changed his life. He was standing in the schoolyard with some friends when a group of older boys drove up in cars. They crashed through a gate, got out of their cars, broke windows in the school, and hurt some boys who were standing nearby. These older boys were in a *clica* (a "club") and called themselves "Thee Mystics."

For protection, Luis, his friend Memo Tovar, and several other sixth graders decided to form their own group. They called it "Thee Impersonations." They thought the Old English word "Thee" made their group sound noble and "bad."

Luis said that he and his friends started their *clica* for many reasons. Luis recalls that at the time, the most important reason the *clica* was formed was to provide them with protection

A mural from the Las Lomas barrio of South San Gabriel in 1970. Luis recalls that gang life was a very big and dangerous part of growing up in the barrio.

against gangs like Thee Mystics. Luis also believes that he and his friends formed the *clica* for the same reasons that other boys might join sports clubs or the Boy Scouts—to have a group to belong to. But Luis also had a dangerous reason for joining: "I wanted the power to [make people afraid]. . . . All my school life until then I was a broken boy, shy and fearful. I wanted what 'Thee Mystics' had; I wanted the power to hurt somebody."

Chapter *Three*

LA VIDA LOCA– AND BEYOND

One hot August day in 1965, when Luis was 11, he came home at dinnertime and found his mother watching the television with a worried expression.

"What's going on, Mama?" Luis asked her.

"Nada, m'ijo ('Nothing, son')," she told him.

But Luis knew that something was wrong. Scenes from Watts, the neighborhood in which they used to live, were being shown on TV. He recognized familiar streets and buildings. Rioters were climbing in and out of the broken windows of stores, police were arresting people, and homes and businesses were on fire.

This was how Luis learned about the Watts Riots, six days of terrible violence that tore through Los Angeles, beginning on August 11, 1965. By the time the riots had ended, nearly 4,000 people were arrested, mostly for stealing. Over 1,000 people were injured, and 34 were killed. Hundreds of buildings were destroyed by fire.

A soldier patrols Luis's former neighborhood in Los Angeles, where riots raged during the summer of 1965.

Although most people in Watts did not riot, the number of rioters was in the thousands. Years of frustrations exploded in a few days of terrible destruction, as desperate people destroyed their own streets and neighborhoods. Luis recalls that the riots made a deep impression on him. "It told me that something was wrong and unfair in the world. It also gave me the idea—which almost ended up killing me—that violence was a way to be heard."

Sixth grade was an unhappy time for Luis. He felt like he wasn't good at anything. Schoolwork was hard for him. So were sports. Whenever classmates chose teams for basketball, he would be the last one picked. He fractured his jaw in a fight with some bullies, and felt embarrassed about how he looked. His jaw healed crookedly, and kids gave him the nickname "Chin."

But Luis did have one accomplishment that made him feel good. He and his brother José got hired to deliver newspapers. Every day after school they would fold the papers and ride their bikes to the houses on the route. Luis got so good at it that he had four routes at once. He would work long hours to make his deliveries, rain or shine.

Luis generally kept to himself and didn't like to talk. But there was one place where he felt at home— when he was with his *clica*, "Thee Impersonations." The group gave Luis a sense of belonging, protection, and respect. At first, it was just a group of boys who would spend free time together in the park or playground. As time went on, though, they began to look for trouble, and they found it. Soon it held them—like flies in a spiderweb.

As Luis entered the eighth grade, he and other members of his group were often caught fighting, destroying school property, and disobeying their teachers. As punishment, the school eventually put the boys in a detention class and kept them apart from the other students. They had to pick up trash and clean graffiti off the walls after school.

He and his friends got in trouble outside of school, too. A boy nicknamed "Yuk Yuk" helped get Luis's group to steal from stores. Yuk Yuk always found someone to buy what they stole. Slowly they were learning to be criminals. Sometimes they got away. Other times they didn't. Security guards would occasionally catch the boys and hold them in the store until their parents came to get them.

Luis's parents were upset when they saw their son getting into trouble. Luis remembers one time when he was seven years old, he took toys and candy from a store and hid them in the closet at home. His mother found everything and made him return what he had stolen to the store.

Luis's father didn't get angry or hit him. That wasn't the kind of man he was. Instead, he challenged Luis to think for himself and question his actions. "You can't be in a fire and not get burned," Mr. Rodriguez told his son. Luis did not know what this meant at first, but as the "fire" of his teenage years

Luis's mother Maria Estela, in Cuidad Juarez, Mexico, during the 1950s.

began to burn hotter and hotter, his father's words echoed in his mind.

In 1967 the Rodriguez family moved again, this time to San Gabriel. Luis entered the Richard Garvey Intermediate School. He started another *clica* there called "Thee Little Gents." The boys in this group drank alcohol and used drugs. An older boy in the neighborhood encouraged them to steal by offering money for what they stole. One day Luis got caught stealing and was arrested for the first time.

The *clicas* were small junior gangs for grade-school kids. When they got older, they joined bigger gangs, such as "Thee Animal Tribe." Being part of these gangs was even more dangerous. Gang members in the older groups used guns and knives in their turf wars with other gangs. Some would die from using drugs or crashing cars while driving drunk.

Luis joined Thee Animal Tribe and soon learned just how dangerous gang life could be. One evening when he and some friends were having a barbecue in the yard of an abandoned house, a car drove by with its headlights turned off. Clavo, one of the members of the group, stretched out his arms and yelled: "Here stand Thee Animal Tribe!"

Two people in the car jumped out and shot at them with an automatic rifle and a sawed-off shotgun. The bullets flew. Everyone hit the ground, and the car sped off down the road and into the hills. Luis's friend Clavo lost his eye to the shotgun blast. Half of

A proud moment for Luis when he returned to his former high school to give a speech to the students.

his face was covered with shotgun pellets and blood.

Surprisingly, the horror of this attack did not discourage Luis and his friends from continuing their gang activity. In fact, it made them pull together.

Luis remembers his friend Memo Tovar calling them all together and making a short speech. "We are all taking a pledge," Memo said, "a pledge to be for each other. Thee Animal Tribe will never let you down. Don't ever let Thee Animal Tribe down."

Luis knew he couldn't let Thee Animal Tribe down. Aside from his family, it was just about all he had in the world.

TO THE EDGE AND BACK

When Luis was 14, he entered Mark Keppel High School in Alhambra. He took mainly industrial arts classes, like woodshop, printshop, and autoshop. Because of low grades, he didn't qualify for the classes that prepared students to go to college. That was fine with him. "I didn't want to have much to do with school. I wanted to be untouchable," Luis recalls. "I walked the halls facing straight ahead. Nobody could get to me."

Later in the year, he was expelled from school for fighting. He also had trouble at home. His parents grew tired of the late-night calls from police stations. His mother, especially, was tired of worrying about him every night. She wouldn't let him live under the family's roof this way. If he couldn't change, she told him, he would have to leave.

Luis chose to run away. He stayed with friends, slept in abandoned cars, and stayed up all night in

Luis has always loved music. Here at age 13, he is learning to play the saxophone at home in San Gabriel.

movie theaters. He had never felt so alone. After a few weeks, he asked his mother if he could come back home. She said he could, but only under new rules. His mother fixed up a small room attached to the garage. This was to be Luis's new room. He was not allowed into the house without her permission. And he had to stay out of trouble. This was his last chance. Luis took it.

During this time, he had stopped going to school and was **initiated** into Las Lomas, the big barrio gang made up from the many smaller *clicas* from all over town. Being a gang member did not solve his problems. He was still bored and unhappy. He was looking for an escape from these feelings. Soon he found one in an activity that he and his fellow gang members called "sniffing spray."

Luis and his friends made spray by soaking a number of **toxic** chemicals into a rag and putting it into a bag. They would then inhale the poisonous fumes from the bag. Spray cut off oxygen to their brains. Luis recalls that spray used to make him dizzy and confused, and he would temporarily forget his problems. But it was extremely dangerous. Sniffing spray meant killing brain cells that could never grow back. As a result, kids sometimes suffered permanent damage or died.

Shortly after the publication of *Always Running*, Luis visits an East L.A. neighborhood. He is standing next to a mural featuring a painting and quote from the famous Mexican revolutionary leader, Emiliano Zapata.

Once while Luis was using spray with friends, he almost did die. He started to dream that he was going through a tunnel and moving toward a bright light. He saw images of all the people in his life. When he came to, he looked up and saw his friends Baba and Wilo. They had taken the spray away from him. He demanded that they give it back. They refused.

"No way," Baba said. "You died, Luis—you stopped breathing and died."

Luis didn't care. That night he wanted to die. "Everything lost its value for me," he remembers. "Death seemed the only door worth opening, the only road toward a future."

Coming so close to death gave Luis a lot to think about. Did he really want to die? Part of him did, but another part of him refused. When he was a little boy left alone in the back of the classroom, he told himself stories, drew pictures, and built with blocks. Now as a teenager he wanted to find ways of expressing how he felt, in art and in writing. Sometimes he painted on the walls of his garage room for hours until every inch was covered. It didn't matter to him if anyone saw it. Making art was just something he had to do.

Another thing he would do alone in his room was write. He wrote stories about the things that happened to him, and he wrote poems. He typed on a manual typewriter that his father had left in the garage. His stories and his feelings were inside him,

Luis addresses youth, community activists, teachers, and law-enforcement groups in Washington, D.C., in the fall of 1994.

and he had to bring them out, whether anyone else read them or not.

In that way, he was like his *Tia* ("Aunt") Chucha. People called her crazy because she used to ride the bus and sing songs at the top of her voice. She would drop in on different members of the family, showing up with a guitar, singing songs, and telling stories. People would poke fun at her, but Luis respected his aunt. Thinking of her gave him the courage to write and create artwork without worrying about what other people would say.

One day Mr. Rothro, the former principal from Luis's elementary school, came for a visit. Mrs. Rodriguez led him into the garage room and left him to talk with Luis. He wanted to encourage Luis to come back to school. He also saw the artwork Luis had painted on the walls. He noticed that Luis had a typewriter and a stack of papers on the bed.

"Luis, you've always struck me as an intelligent young man," Mr. Rothro said. "But your mother tells me you're wasting away your days. I'd like to see you back in school. Promise me you'll think about it."

At the same time, other people came into Luis's life who helped give him confidence in himself and his abilities. In the years after the Watts Riots, government grants helped provide community services around Los Angeles. The Bienvenidos Community Center opened in South San Gabriel and offered tutoring, job placement, day care, and a safe place for young people to be together.

The staff of the Bienvenidos Community Center had grown up in the neighborhood and were dedicated to helping the community improve itself. They gave Luis and other young people opportunities to make money picking up trash from the parks and helping bring food from the market to hungry families. Eventually, Luis got a chance to use his artistic talent. He was given materials and training to paint murals in the community.

Luis recalls that several people at the Center played an important role in his life. "There were a few guys at the Center that I looked up to. They didn't need to act bad to operate. They knew how to handle themselves and be strong, intelligent, and in control.

They could influence me without judging me or telling me what to do. They were just there. They listened, and if I was wrong about something, before they would say anything, they would get me to think.

"I remember one dude that had a big influence on me. I was telling him how I had to defend the neighborhood against our gang's enemies no matter what the cost. He put a small globe in my hand and asked me where South San Gabriel was on the globe. I found the United States, then little California, then a tiny dot which was Los Angeles, but there was no

Volunteers pitch in to help clean and restore neighborhoods after the Los Angeles riots in 1992.

South San Gabriel, no Las Lomas barrio—it was too small. To me Las Lomas was everything, but when you get outside it, it's too small to see, too small to die for, that's for sure."

Encouraged by teachers at the Center, Luis started to think for himself and see the world in a new way. They encouraged him to return to school and become involved in community work. He learned to help out, to use his artistic talents, and to become a leader. A few of his friends from the gang did not approve of what he was doing, but Luis was now getting encouragement from outside of the gang. Slowly, Luis started to think about returning to school. He was beginning to see the world as a bigger place, one where he could feel important by making a contribution to his community.

THE POWER IS WITHIN YOU

In the fall of 1970, Luis stood on the edge between his old life and his new one. Though he was ready to learn and discover his creative abilities, he still hadn't left *La Vida Loca*.

"There are two sides inside of all of us," he wrote at the time. "One that will allow us to do very evil things, and the other which will let us express a lot of love. Sometimes the world nudges one side of us, sometimes it nudges the other. But in the end, we can decide which one we will play with."

Luis returned to school at the age of 16. People at the community center supported his decision and offered him tutoring and encouragement. "I picked up things easily, and that helped. They believed in me and helped convince me that I was smart. No one had treated me that way before. It changed the way I thought of myself and what I could do."

At Keppel High School, Luis joined a student

Even at an early age, Luis had strong political and activist opinions. At age 16, this picture of Luis was taken following his arrest in the 1970 Chicano Moratorium Against the Vietnam War.

group called "To Help Mexican-American Students" (ToHMAS). This group wanted to convince the principal and teachers to pay more attention to Mexican culture and history. After all, almost half the Keppel students were Mexican American.

Luis had never thought of himself as a good speaker, but when he spoke at ToHMAS meetings, students listened. They respected the power of his words and feelings. They looked to him as a leader. They pushed him forward in ways he would never have tried himself.

For example, in 1971, ToHMAS asked Luis to represent Mexican-American students in a school-wide competition. The school held a contest to choose who would get to be "Joe and Josephine Aztec," Indian warrior characters from ancient Mexico who would be the school's mascots at football games. Luis and other students felt that the clownish antics of former mascots showed disrespect to Mexican-American students and their heritage.

Members of ToHMAS asked Luis and a female classmate to represent them and perform traditional Aztec dances. The students wanted to promote dignity and respect for Mexican culture. "If it was up to me entirely, I never would have done it," Luis recalls, "but I was willing to try." Luis and his partner performed traditional dances and won the competition.

Luis became well known throughout the school. He also became more confident. Later that year, he

One of the great influences on Luis's life was writer Claude Brown, author of *Manchild in the Promised Land*. Brown is shown here, testifying at a government hearing on the problems affecting young people in American cities.

became the president of ToHMAS and was asked by the local school board to join them as a student representative.

Luis continued to write. He spent hours typing poems and stories. When several teachers read his work, one asked if she could enter his writing in a contest sponsored by the Quinto Sol publishing house. This contest was meant to discover and encourage young writers by offering them a chance at publication. At first Luis refused to enter his manuscript because he was embarrassed by all the mistakes in it. The teacher told him not to let mistakes stop him. When you have something to say, you should always feel free to get it onto paper. You can always fix it afterward, she told him.

The teacher helped Luis retype the manuscript and fix the mistakes. Gradually, he learned how to do this for himself. Luis's skill and confidence continued to grow until he had his own column in the school newspaper. He called it *Pensamientos,* which means "thoughts."

Like all good writers, Luis had also learned by reading other books. He especially liked *Down These Mean Streets,* a story of street life in New York City, by Piri Thomas. Luis loved this book because it described a life like his own and made it something the world could see. Some of his other favorite authors were Claude Brown, Victor Hernandez Cruz, and Ricardo Sanchez, all of whom wrote about city and barrio life in a truthful and realistic way.

In June 1972 Luis graduated from high school. He received his diploma and made his parents proud. He had accomplished a lot but was only beginning to reach for his dreams.

The manuscript that he had sent off to the Quinto Sol competition had turned out to be a prizewinner! The publisher called Luis to congratulate him. The prize was $250, a contract to publish his book, and a plane ticket to San Francisco. Luis couldn't believe it. His heart danced. This was more money than he had ever earned at one time. He had never flown in an airplane before. This was the greatest thing that ever happened to anyone he knew. He threw his arms into the air and shouted for joy.

Luis's life was changing, but just when things were beginning to look their brightest, he had a huge setback. He was outside a club late one night and saw police officers trying to unjustly arrest someone. He yelled at them to stop and ended up in a scuffle with them. They arrested him and charged him with assaulting an officer. Luis found himself locked up in the Los Angeles County Jail, facing a possible six-year sentence.

Luis felt crushed. When he was in jail before, he had nothing to lose. This time jail meant giving up his dreams of going to college and being a writer. It meant letting down the people who believed in him.

To his surprise teachers, friends, and people from the community center wrote letters to the judge on

Luis with his son
Ruben in 1993.

his behalf. "If I didn't have people seeing something in
me that I couldn't see, I would have gone back to my old
ways," Luis says. The faith everyone showed helped convince
the judge that Luis should have another chance. He got
out of prison after ten long weeks.

Luis refused to fall back into *La Vida Loca*. Before he
left his jail cell, he made a solemn vow. He promised
himself never again to be involved in gangs, take drugs,
or end up back in jail for a criminal offense. Almost 25
years later, he has kept true to each part of his vow.

Chapter Six

THIS IS NOT JUST FOR ME

As an adult, Luis J. Rodriguez has accomplished a great deal. He has written award-winning books and appeared before millions of people on television and radio. He has spoken to people in more than 60 cities throughout the United States and Europe. He has become a book publisher and a magazine and newspaper commentator. Who could have predicted that Luis Rodriguez of Las Lomas and Thee Animal Tribe would have gone on to do so much?

When Luis was young, he was angry and felt a lack of connection to other people. This changed when he found his ability to express himself and when people started to respect him for his talents. He discovered the power of his voice and learned how to make a difference with it.

After high school Luis went to work in a factory to earn money. In the evenings he would write poems and stories. He also applied to a special training program for journalists at the University of California at Berkeley. At first he was rejected, but as Luis recalls, "I was persistent and I kept sending them letters and bugging them. They saw how badly I wanted to be in the program, and they finally accepted me. This led to me getting my first job as a reporter."

Luis was married for a brief time. He and his wife, Camila, had two children named Ramiro and Andrea, but the marriage eventually ended in divorce.

In 1985 he moved to Chicago, where there were better opportunities for him to be a journalist. He was able to write stories describing the problems of homeless people and unemployed factory workers.

Luis at age 22 with his first wife Camila, and their first son, Ramiro, in Los Angeles in 1976.

In Chicago he flourished both professionally and personally. In 1988 he married Maria Trinidad Cardenas. They first met while working on a newspaper together. Several years later they had a baby boy, Ruben Joaquin.

In the daytime Luis worked as a typesetter. On weekends he was a reporter for an all-news radio station. In the evening he continued to write poetry and even read it aloud in theaters and clubs. He wanted to publish his work and began sending it to large publishers in New York and elsewhere. They all turned him down. But Luis did not give up. Friends encouraged him to apply for a grant. A grant is money that comes from a business or the government that goes to artists who have

By 1995 Luis had moved to Chicago. He is shown here with his second wife, Trini, and their sons, Luis Jacinto and Ruben.

produced good work that needs support. In 1989 Luis won grants from the city of Chicago and the state of Illinois. He used this money to publish his book himself. He called it *Poems Across the Pavement.*

To publish his book, he started his own company. He named it "Tia Chucha Press" after his story-telling aunt who had inspired him as a boy. (Tia Chucha Press is now a successful publishing house.) This book won the Poetry Center Book Award from San Francisco State University. Winning this award was a great step forward for Luis.

Luis's second book of poetry, *The Concrete River,* also won an award in 1991. At the time it was published, his teenage son Ramiro (who had come from California to live with him) had joined a gang and was getting into trouble at school. Luis decided that his next book, which he named *Always Running,* would be the story of his own life. As a father he wanted to write a book that would help and inspire his children.

As it turned out, in April 1992, as he worked on *Always Running,* parts of the city of Los Angeles once again erupted into violence and riots. Many people throughout the nation focused on the problems that had led to these days of destruction. Because Luis had written a poetic and truthful book, many people looked to him and his story for understanding. He became an important voice for young people facing the problems of growing up in American cities.

Luis is now 42 years old and lives in Chicago with

his wife Trini, daughter Andrea, and sons Ramiro, Ruben, and Luis Jacinto. His gang days are half a lifetime behind him, but the problems of young people are never far from his mind.

"Having kids and seeing what they have to deal with keeps me aware. As a father I want to do something. I know that the best gift that I have to offer is my ability to write. I want to somehow use my writing to help make things better for my own kids and all kids," he says.

Luis has used his talents as a writer and speaker to help build understanding between adults and teenagers. In writing about his own life, Luis has helped illustrate what is happening to thousands of others who may never get to write a book.

Some people argue that the solutions to the problems of gangs, violence, and drug abuse are to have more police and more jails. Luis disagrees.

"A lot of young people feel that they are living in a world where there is no place for them," Luis says. "There are no adults there for them to show them how they are supposed to make it through. And it can be very dangerous out there."

Luis has tried to heal the problems of gang violence directly. He has taken part in events such as the National Gang Peace Summit in El Paso, Texas, in 1995. He is also one of the founders of a Chicago-based organization called Youth Struggling for Survival, which brings together parents, teachers, and

Christmas 1995 in the Rodriguez home in Chicago. Ramiro is pictured at the bottom left, and Luis's daughter, Andrea, appears at the top right.

youth in an attempt to find solutions to the problems affecting young people.

"We are living in a difficult time," Luis says, "but it offers tremendous opportunities. We have to help kids see that there's a bigger world out there. They need to be valued and accepted so they can contribute their gifts to the world. With technology we have all kinds of tools for expression that didn't exist before. We have to help kids find and unleash their power. Creativity and expression are the future."

Important Dates

1954   Born in El Paso, Texas, on July 9.

1956   Rodriguez family moves to Los Angeles.

1965   Joins a *clica*, or youth gang.

1973   Held in L.A. County jail. Vows never to take drugs, be involved in gangs, or go to jail again. Studies journalism, and continues to write poetry.

1974   Marries Camila Martinez.

1975   Son Ramiro is born.

1977   Daughter Andrea is born.

1980   Works as a journalist.

1985   Moves to Chicago. Is a reporter and newspaper editor.

1988- Marries Maria Trinidad Cardenas. Son Ruben is born.
1989   Founds Tia Chucha Press and publishes *Poems Across the Pavement.*

1991   Publishes *The Concrete River.*

1992   Riots in Los Angeles occur after the police are found innocent in the beating of motorist Rodney King.

1993   *Always Running* is published. Becomes a cofounder of Youth Struggling for Survival, in Chicago.

1994   Son Luis Jacinto is born.

1996   Continues writing, speaking, working with youth organizations, and running Tia Chucha Press.

Glossary

barrio   A Spanish word, meaning "neighborhood."

initiation   The procedure for being accepted into a group.

La Vida Loca   A Spanish phrase that literally means "The Crazy Life" and refers to life in barrio gangs.

toxic   Poisonous.

Bibliography

Hernandez, Irene Beltran. *The Secret of Two Brothers.* Piñata Books (Arte Publico Press), 1995.

Mohr, Nicholasa. *All for the Better: A Story of El Barrio.* Raintree Steck-Vaughn, 1992.

Ponce, Mary Helen. *Hoyt Street: An Autobiography.* University of New Mexico Press, 1993.

Rodriguez, Luis J. *Poems Across the Pavement.* Tia Chucha Press, 1989.

Rodriguez, Luis J. *The Concrete River.* Curbstone Press, 1991.

Rodriguez, Luis J. *Always Running La Vida Loca: Gang Days in L.A.* Touchstone, 1994.

Soto, Gary. *Living Up the Street.* Dell, 1992.

Index